AWAY WITH WORDS

AN ANTHOLOGY OF POETRY

AERONWY THOMAS   BERYL MYERS
ANNIE TAYLOR   FRANCES WHITE

Aeronwy Thomas

Illustrated by

Annie Taylor & Beryl Myers

© The Authors 2007

Poetry Monthly Press

Cover Design

© Annie Taylor

© The Authors 2007

CONTENTS

Conflict and Harmony

Light and Dark

Time and Transition

Last words

INTRODUCTION

Just a word - can we do without them! - about the contributors to this anthology: Annie, Beryl, Frances and myself, Aeronwy. We've known each other from twenty to forty years - enough time to know each other's works, their strengths and sometime weaknesses.

We meet on a regular basis to encourage each other and make tentative "suggestions" for improvements. When we change or delete a word or line, it is usually in the interests of clarity and simplicity. Of course, we don't always follow each other's advice if we feel it might unbalance the rest of the poem. As we dissect each other's offerings, we take time (lots of it) to communicate family and personal triumphs and disasters.

Over the years, we've become like fruit on the vine, maturing nicely in each other's company, though not yet ripe enough to fall.

Aeronwy Thomas

EAGLE

The eagle soars above the mountain.
From his view the mountain is a mountain.
For us below, clouds obscure the summit.
The eagle dips below the cloud.
The mountain is not a mountain.
Soaring above again,
the mountain is a mountain.
Be watchful, the situation is in the eye
of the beholder.

Aeronwy Thomas

SEAGULL

Sea gull, free gull
Strutting in the car park
Colour coded with the asphalt
White on Grey

Sea gull, free gull
Are you on the level
Have you left the seaside
For an urban holiday

Did you come up river
On the oily swelling tide
Clocked a passing fishing boat
Hitched a lazy ride

Seagull, free gull
Have you done a runner
Bored with rollercoaster waves
And candyfloss spray

Sea gull, free gull
Strutting in the car park
Tired of the home game
Playing away

Annie Taylor

PEACOCKS

A flowering of peacocks: blue
turquoise, electric, royal,
pale and dark, greeny blue.
Until I saw a peacock,
I thought blue was only
one colour.

Aeronwy Thomas

URBAN FOX

In the ever bright, Ever Ready light city night
overwhelming moon-phases and star gazers,
the Amber Gambler, Jack of Napes, Scapegrace,
nimble as Fred Astaire. White tied,
red tailed, paled by the sodium glare.

Captain Scarlett, Masked Stranger, Lone Ranger,
Louche Scaramouche, Cool foot Luke.
Duke of Dustbins, King of Catch-as-catch can,
Frontier Man. Country Cousin
now City slicker, none quicker on the paw.

Lurking in alleys, dodging sallies.
a Who-dun-it Houdini
now you see me - now, in the blink
of a sly eye, by sleight of feet,
Gone!   Not to earth - but concrete!

Annie Taylor

HERON

Still as death he stands
cloaked in misty grey
Silently he waits
purposeful
bright eyes alert
Sudden strike and splash
a second's silver gleam
the hunter's stance resumed
The stream runs on

Beryl Myers

PET SHOP

Sweet smell of sawdust
and puppies
tickle my nose
a scratching
against the cage
scrapes my ears
snakes
slithering
no hurry
furtive
the shop owner
surveys his prey
touch of notes
I part with
for the gecko
last chance
release him
to cold and cats
talking of which
I'll take
that black and white
one eye open
to see me
choosing
through the bars.

Time to go
they're all here
for good
or worse.

Aeronwy Thomas

OPEN THE GATE

Open the cage
let the parakeet out
suburban gardens
woodland parks

Pour the fish bowl
down the drain
the sewer
ocean wave

Leave the garden gate
unlatched
dogs walk out
birds sing

Open
the night window
let the stars in.

Aeronwy Thomas

SONNET TO J.S.B.

I love the brilliant certainty of Bach,
His perfect pitch within his Universe.
Where Reason leitmotifs discordant dark,
With ordered Intervals where minds converse.
His bright vibrations tune the strings of Time,
Untarnished by the fetid breath of days
Of Disonance. And Harmony and Rhyme
Repair the melody the piper plays.
Is Life a Fugue of round-recurring measure?
Or just crescendoed, ill-cacophanies?
Do we exist, mere accidents of pleasure,
Or broken Chords that never found their keys?
How change the burden of ill-tempered years,
To yet restore the Music of the Spheres?

Annie Taylor

YELLOW SONNET

Yellow, yellow, yell out loud.
Tell me that's a lemon cloud.
Either you are telling lies
or having trouble with your eyes.

Does that ring I gave to you
show its worth in golden hue?
No, don't be a silly arse
...a curtain ring, it's made of brass.

Mustard seems to mar my sight.
Is a jaundiced view my plight?
NO, neither is it yellow fever.
Just some trouble with my liver.

Caused, I am inclined to think
by YOU...You`re driving me to drink.

Beryl Myers

SEA DRAGON

Deep in the ocean where no one can see
I'm as green and as green as green can be,
with eyes of gold
and a tongue bright blue,
with crystal teeth
and a frilly crest too,
a real cool dragon that's me.

My home is a cave in the coral below.
Around the door anemones grow.
I don't belch fire
and I don't have fights.
I never snore
when asleep at nights.
I breathe green bubbles that glow.

When fish and lobsters visit me
I offer them biscuits and cups of tea.
I don't eat boys
and I don't eat girls.
I feed on weed
and occasional pearls.
I'm a vegan dragon you see.

Beryl Myers

MUREX BRANDARIS

A creeping mollusc,
a spiral shell.
Once it was dragged from the sea
for its purple dye
so highly prized in the eyes of the mighty
to colour the hems of their togas,
to denote their wealth and status.
Thousands of harmless fish died for this.
Such is the pride of men.

Royal Purple – The colour of Kings.
Adorned in rich materials, gold and jewels,
they parade their pomp, revel in their glory.
The panoply of power
before which the hoipolloi must bow.
Yet, for all their majesty
these Caesars, then and now,
never could compare
with the beauty of the shell.

Beryl Myers

SWIFTSCAPE

Swifts dive and screech
flying low behind the trees
chasing gnats in the warm air.

Only a wisp of moon
an innuendo in the clear blue sky
as their silhouettes rise and swoop.

They dart away down streets
like rowdy bikers
revelling in each twist and turn

to reappear screaming
on scimitar wings
cutting black arcs across the sky.

As swifts outfly the shadows
jasmine fills the air
a blackbird sings, safe in the cherry tree.

Hushed, they wheel and spiral higher
gliding sky-skaters tracing patterns
round the moon.

I gaze until their soaring shapes
merge into the soft mid-summer night
and darkness breaks the spell.

Frances White

LLWYNPERDID FARM

Trusted with the farmer's new ponies
ungroomed and hardly broken-in
my brother and I trembled at their white eyes rolling
as the heavy slap of saddle and clink of bridle
sealed our fate.

Bare headed
only the whack of a leaf stripped fern for mastery
we were released from the farmyard
clattering on stony lanes
up through the pine forest
to a long range on the mountain top.

There, in a wind whipped frenzy
they sidestepped and pranced
till we gave rein and raced for miles
on that boundless horizon of grass and sky
hooves thundering, rhythmic, concentrated
legs invisibly stretching into flight
wild and free above valley and pit
might, mane, and tail
disappearing like a meteor over Rhondda.

Frances White

WALL JUMPERS

"Damned wall jumpers in Top Pasture!"
He'd noted they weren't all his sheep
and went back after supper
to sort them out.
No moon, his boots sunk
as he leant into the lower slopes
behind the farmhouse.

He climbed over gate and stile, calling
"Here Meg".
The collie circled the perimeter, sniffing
for treats of afterbirth. In the silence
new lambs were being born
steaming on the cold hillside
to survive or not
he wouldn't know till dawn
but now
he was tracking trespassers.

No sign, till he reached a sheltered hollow
by the last gate onto open fell
and startled a band of ewes.
They thundered in an avalanche over limestone rocks
the white outcrop just discernible.
He'd missed cornering them and cursed
striding down the slope, shouting for the dog.
"To heel! Come in a hint!"
They bolted this way and that, frantic
to escape the collie, as she darted
through the dark and crouched, panting.

Stones tumbled when they breached the wall.
He followed through and set to, rebuilding
securing his boundary with fallen slabs
blocking the way he'd come. He knew
another way back, steeper, more slippery
so pitch black, he couldn't see his feet.

"That was a tricky one, eh Meg?
And a torch would've been a good idea."

Frances White

BEFORE AND AFTER CHILDREN

Before children...
You heap your bed with Cutie Bears and Sassy dolls
Your lover gives you bunnies in designer t-shirts
With 'I wuve yu' on the front.
Your kittens are named 'Miss Purry Paws', 'Sock-it-to-me-Sam'
And 'Tussie Mussie'.
In the confines of your Lifestyle
You are mildly concerned with crimewaves
But comforted by 'Neighbourhood Watch'.
Aware of mugging, you carry mace in your handbag
In case of terrorism on the tube, you imput ICE on your mobile phone.
Pondering natural disasters over 'after eights'
You assess averages, discuss statistics, weigh up probabilities,
And change the subject...
On the slippery slopes of Love,
You are careful not to lose your balance,
Wearing your heart on your sleeve
You cover it with a cardigan.

After children…
Tsunamis sweep up the Thames, there's a maelstrom at Putney
Scylla and Charybdis lurk under Hammersmith bridge
The San Andreas fault opens in Chiswick High street.
Out of a clear blue sky, Jumbo jets fall like comets
Comets crash like hailstones
Bears spring from pavement cracks
Urban Guerrillas masquerade as Lollypop Ladies
'Jack the Ripper's great great grandson prowls Paddington Station
The newsagents hides a Paedophile Ring.
You know the worst that could possibly happen…often does,
And will for certain the moment your back is turned.
After children
You'd gladly die for love
And never forgive yourself for going.

Annie Taylor

LULLABY

They told me I must say goodbye.
His birth was long and I was torn
but I still sing his lullaby.

He did not breathe. He did not cry.
I held him close to keep him warm.
They told me I must say goodbye.

Above white masks, they glanced awry.
In vain, I breathed into his form
but still I sang him lullaby.

They gave no answer to my, Why.
The guilt was theirs who would not mourn
and told me I must say goodbye.

You must forgive, they seemed to sigh.
My heart was with the hushed new-born
I rocked in tender lullaby.

Now every May when swallows fly
white blossoms spread among the thorn.
They told me I must say goodbye
but I still sing his lullaby.

Frances White

NEWBORN

My pink alien
from inner space,
coiled in the seed and sprung
like surprises at Christmas,
dumpling-wrapped and damp.
Bossman.

Siren yells summon
whirligigs in my gut.
Swamp-frog
in my fairy tale dream album,
a snapshot Prince.

Beryl Myers

MARCH HARE

The day you kick started
March clouds billowed
catkins yellowed
lambs-tails leapt on hazel boughs
ten months on
you make your stand
find your form
stamping out your chosen ground

Forge your rhythm
heart beating
foot fleeting
to and fro-ing coming going
the house rocks and rolls
floors creak
crocks clink
kitchen clocks clack and ping

Each time you leave
tap shoes
mark the blues
shuffle softly in sad corners
boots bent to your toes
heel over
sneakers hover
ballet slippers block the stairs

When at last
you cast your reels
show your heels
touch wood, not too soon
leave me a measure
of moted traces
stirring the places
where you danced your tune.

Annie Taylor

SCHOOL DINNER

Today, as usual, we sit
struggling to swallow.
On the first floor,
tables covered in green oil-cloth
dinner ladies ladle dollops
of sloppy veg, suspect mince
onto plain white plates.
Wartime nourishment.
No meat in the mince.
No sugar in the sweet.

An engine roars,
stutter of gunfire.
I look up at the window,
see the plane coming at us.
It rises,
shows its underbelly.
Black crosses on each wing tip.

Its over,
soaring overhead,
over in seconds.
No time for fear.
We were lucky, the bullets missed us.
Another school
was bombed.

Beryl Myers

GYPSY

Plum picking time.
He had come to school
in his new shoes,
learnt to write his name.
I had seen his home,
a painted caravan,
camped amongst bushes,
a skinny dog tied up with cord,
a skewbald horse champing
the rough grass
beside the road.

Curious, I had longed
to see inside.
"Just a peep" I begged.
The dark woman in long skirts
stood atop the steps,
opened the door.
I might look but not enter
(mud on my boots),
see her bright curtains,
her polished stove, gleaming.
I was overcome,
dumb with admiration.

Beryl Myers

DANDELION CHILD

Dandelion child
down the back alley
playing with boys
in the dirt and gravel
laughing, shouting
shrieking in the sunshine
safe
between gardens
in quiet shadows
gathering brash
ragged blooms
to fill jam jars
in the kitchen.

Lily white adolescence
clean dresses
shy wonder
at the willowherb
towering where we walked
by the railway track
a lull
before hot summers
the rush of freedom
music in the air
wild flowers in our hair
and then the longing
for red roses.

Frances White

BLOOMS FOR THE BRIDE

So after all these years you're set to wed
and April is the perfect month to choose
when colours waver between blue and red.

A lady so determined not to lose
could opt for flowers to match a purple gown
and devastate the nation on the News.

I do not see you veiled but with a crown
of Hellebore and swaying Lupin plumes.
Snakeshead Fritillary bells hang down

from your bouquet of Rhododendron blooms.
A Bella Donna garter round your limb
will test the agile fingers of your groom

when you draw the deadly shades around and grin
tonight as you slither into bed with him.

Frances White

WITHOUT WHICH

The catalogues all tell me
I must have this and that
I need a scratching post it seems
for my lazy daisy cat.

The essential this week's fashion
is what can not be missed
I must put the crazy latest
on my vital shopping list.

The offers come in drifts
on the mat before my door
for pizzas that I hate
and freebies I abhor.

The telephone keeps ringing
to tell of double-glazing
or insurance that is cheaper
when the only thing I'm needing
is a volunteer housekeeper.

Beryl Myers

VENUS OBSERVED

Jupiter! This mirror's heavy!
on the back it says
'Secondhand Heaven – Portobello Road'
I know the place
it's full of beds and mirrors
chaise longues and velvet curtains.
We go there when we're down
on our uppers, mum and me
velvet's classy and kind to the pussy
She's lying here waiting for customers
assessing her assets – taking a breather
before the next blow by blow.
Well it's a living – keeps you indoors
I fly around a bit, keep the place tidy
make myself scarce – we are pretty scarce
we boys with wings - 'featherlite' you
might say. We do a bit of bondage
blue for a boy – pink for a girl
you kinda get caught up in it.

Annie Taylor

PINK FLUFF

A bit of pink fluff
tied round
a long blond
pony tail
gold ring
piercing her nose
small tattoo
rose-madder tights
this catwalk flamingo
struts from the gloom
catching the spotlight
through the tobacco smoke
gaudy, gorgeous
pulling the beery gaze
of Rizla guys
old as her Dad.

Rhythm 'n' Blues
thumps out its rumpus
on the makeshift stage.
Everyone moves
swings loose
forgets the day
as the nightclub rocks
'n' the beat holds sway.

Frances White

WAITING

In the street light's sulphur glow
a silhouetted form
stands waiting
shine of blonded hair
glint of earrings
hint of fear
Black limmo creeps
stops near
She does a deal
steps in
is gone
Her scarf shines golden
on the unforgiving stone.

Beryl Myers

OLD WOMAN WITH GOLDEN HAIR

old woman with golden hair
breakwatering Time
with siren locks
telling a Lorelei
fishing for compliments

old woman with red mouth
upfronting Death
with puckered provocation
Scarlett O'Horror
fangs ain't what they used to be

old woman in short skirt
outstripping Years
with raunchy haunches
Fanny by Gaslight
too late for show business

old woman in high heels
reaching for Youth
with fallen arches
Gloria Swansong
teetering into the sunset

Annie Taylor

THE PARASOL

Today I saw you
on the sunny side
of the road
smiling and waving
high heels clicking
a pedestrian bumped you
and you crossed
to join me the other side
in a pool of gloom –
I shouldn't have spoken
about Mother's death –
made you remember
an urgent appointment
escaping in the nick of time
from the shady side
to enjoy the rest of the day
in full sun
a parasol to protect you
from its overpowering rays.

Aeronwy Thomas

MARY DIBBLE

Where are you lying, MARY DIBBLE of SOMERSET
in the churchyard of St Giles that exists no longer
in The Ward of Cripplegate Without
Not beneath your tombstone that's for sure!
It has been re-sited, and, face upward
conjoined with others in a pleasant pavement pattern
signifying nothing greater than a picnic place.
All the same, magnolia petals flutter down
smelling of warm, exotic, distant places
and caress the tired letters of your name.
No less white and fragrant were the apple blossoms
swathing the gentle valleys of your youth in rural Somerset
far from The Ward of Cripplegate Without.

Annie Taylor

BLUEBELLS

I don't care much for bluebells now
though once I used to long
for them each year
to sweep their misty veils
beneath the beeches
below the leaping green
and in between the grey-ghost trunks
filling the empty spaces.

I saw my baby brother only once
inside his cage of glass
soft as a moth
a creature of the dusk
no flush of dawn upon his cheek
nor hollow on the pillow
just a bruised and fleeting shadow
brushing the empty space.

I picked a million bluebells for my mother
"they smell of spring" she said
her smile traversed
a mile of winter
she pressed their drooping heads
against her breast
filling the space inside her grey-ghost arms
the empty space.

Annie Taylor

CITY TREE

Lopped
the tree outside my bedroom
shows
knobbles on stumps
fists without fingers
not a pretty sight.

When I first moved here
in the flush of marriage vows
I chose this house
with the city tree
a canopy of green
for birds and humans.
Yes, I'll have you, I said.

A dead branch here
another too close and more
that might fall
on our neighbour's car,
our tree spreads its leaves
every spring.

My nuptial years
survived
we pruned discreetly
errors, secrets, habits
my teeth decay
his hair falls out
the body of marriage
intact.

We struggle on
loyalties stronger

than in the splendour
of early days
when our city tree
spread green
each spring.

Aeronwy Thomas

NASTURTIUMS

Nasturtiums trail in autumn light
as summer's height
softly closes.
Frail roses
dwindle on the broken trellis.

It was true bliss
to sit with you
although we knew
our sun-baked terracotta days
were final rays
to compensate
your wasting state.

Frances White

FINAL FLUTTER

My brother
and cousin
turned grey
at the end
an overenjoy
wrong pleasures
gambling
drinking
accumulating
in excess
books, property
debts
strangely
ever sociable
they arranged
last meetings
last meals
my cousin's
in a Greek
restaurant
where we placed
our bets
for the Grand National
my brother's
a last Christmas
with family
for November
but he died in October
grey
on a beautiful
blue sky day.

Aeronwy Thomas

MOON

I cry to the winds
hear no answer
cry all night
the stars are cold
beg for your arms
you hug yourself.
The moon waxes
and wanes
never grows warmer.

Aeronwy Thomas

ICY VALENTINE

As the North wind blows
I'll woo with Purple prose
My Icy Valentine

Lips bruised mauve
Breathe Eternal Love
In desperate rhyme

Glacial fingers still
Rigid with Winter chill
Pen each aching line

Jack Frost Lover
Lost to Spring forever
Frozen for all time

Annie Taylor

BEE

Like a trapped soul,
the bee on the window pane
drones impatiently -
a buzz of anguish,
as he flings himself
vainly against the glass.

At the telephone, a man,
idly talking, hears
this irritation in his mind;
opens the window gently.

Once more the bee throws all
his featherweight at the window;
but now - stunned, with wings
working in natural motion -
he finds freedom, flies away.

The man closes the window,
satisfied:
he would do the same for his brother
or sister.

Aeronwy Thomas

FOR MYFANWY

You come to the gate to meet us
your feet on the sturdy gravel
treading as though on quicksands
keeping the gauzy air so still around you
no leaf remarks your presence; nor petal falls

With concentrated precision you hold erect
I have seen that intent balance
in tightrope walkers
their bodies centred with minute exactness
weighing Gravity and Grave

I embrace you with desperate care
afraid to press, to hold, to tilt
such fragile equilibrium
My husband, more impetuous that I
gives you the hug I'm terrified to risk

Our deliberately insouciant conversation
hops about, like sparrows in a branchy bush
We take our social reflection
from your eyes, probing no deeper
than you, or us, can bear

We respect your façade of ordinariness
and play your version of 'Truth, Dare and Promise'
like obedient children
We are in your hands, and their circle
tailors our perimeters

The back of my throat aches
with the force of pent-up wishing. Silent pleading
that the evidence be disallowed
the jury re-consider
the verdict be indefinitely suspended.

Annie Taylor

PAST LOVE

We touch hands briefly in greeting
Kiss hands with social enthusiasm
Hug lightly under the gaze of friends
Never under covers.
We sit on separate sides
Pressed only against the same table
Sharing cloth and condiments
Guarding our knives and forks.

We play at different games
Holding our lives in front of our faces
Defending our choices
Hiding the threes, showing the aces.
Breath is no longer for holding
Time is not precious to us
Neither endless nor urgent
Clock hands do not rush or creep.

We are indifferent to proximity
When our eyes meet, fleetingly
Their irises keep bright blue or brown
Like well painted front doors.
But, is there a flicker in the space between us
A dazzle, leaves against a window pane
Faint throbbing of a migraine,
Last remnants of an ache of heart.

Annie Taylor

ASHES

Those luscious lips gave
kissing scores to eager boys
brave apprentices.
Her fiancé now holds against
his broken heart her ashes.
Remains
impersonal
outrageously refined
fiery passion extinguished
a s h e s.

Frances White

DAISIES AND BOTTLEBRUSH

It's growing old.
Fifty years gone since it`s roots
first twisted round our hearts.
Green shoots of giggles, secrets shared,
teenage bubbles floating free,
pops of disappointment, crushes,
flirting safe in doubles,
breathing in the spring where daisies grew.

Still a sapling, it was split in two,
forced unwillingly apart.
The ripping left us raw, sap running,
fearing the gap between too great.
Now spanning half the world, healed and grown
as siamese twins joined at the feet.

There kangaroos leap, nibble by bottlebrush,
clouds breathe scent of gum trees over oceans.
Here the fallow deer browse,
nose deep in clover.
Seasonal leaves are blown, criss-cross;
their lines informing, form a constant bond.
Picture cards of Melbourne, Wagga Wagga,
Rosebud and mimosa.
Photos keeping pace with weddings.
New faces for our albums.
How quickly we become ... mums and grandmas.

How many frosty winters in my boots
and mitts I thought of you
laid out bikinied on a beach, hot,
with the turkey, the trimmings and the rest, even
the Christmas pudding draped in cream
and topped with plastic holly.

While I had never seen your Southern Cross
above my head and thirty years of more had passed
before you stood again
beneath the Pole-Star of your birth,
I waited anxiously ... a stranger or a friend?
Ageing branches bend to touch
as we embrace.
The rustlings of our thoughts burst into words.
No time had passed.

Beryl Myers

ARUM

Is
love
like an
arum lily
virgin white
hiding beneath
the hedgerows in
deep shady places
holding blood red
berries to tempt
yet poison
any who
dare
to
t
a
s
t
e
?

Beryl Myers

FOUNTAIN

                    Is
                   love
                  like the
                   sand that fountains
                 from dunes on
               a windy day
              to grit and
             dumb the
            tongue
           blind
          eyes,
         hide
        the
       T
       r
       u
       t
       h
       ?

Beryl Myers

BACK TO UNIVERSITY

Poinsettia extends its wings,
you pack your things.
New year awaits
at student gates.

Along the motorway you speed
with all you need,
PC, CDs,
we pay the fees.

I slowly start to strip your bed,
"Bye, Mum," you said.
Despite your height
I hugged you tight.

Frances White

BLUE

Blue
that
is
what
I'm
feeling
and
you
what
are
you
feeling
now
you're
going
your
way
and
I'm
going
mine.
Blue

Aeronwy Thomas

THE WIRELESS SET

It keeps its place beside his fireside chair
voice sonorous - bass soft with hint of bumblebee
treble clipped but clear
tone polished as the beechwood case
the speaker cover slightly torn behind the fretted filigree
worn by vibrations of a lifetime's air.

Built to navigate an older ordered sea
ride measured waves - find distant ports
with certain clarity
now baffled by electric storms
its ancient charts are useless - compass gone - words drown
in whirlpools of cacophony.

I guide his hand - and we're on course again
"Thank you, dear old Peg" he says
it's my mother's name......

Annie Taylor

LETTER FROM MOUNTAIN ASH

Funeral's over.
Now I've cleared my sister's flat
keys go back to warden.

Took some flowers up –
the mountain thick with mist!
Left the grave tidy.

Kept some things of hers.
You can take a vase or brooch
next time you stay.

You kids from London
loved running down the valley
singing our Welsh songs.

Only me left now.
A big family we were
here in Mountain Ash.

This rain never stops.
I miss my coal fire's flicker –
must call chimney sweep.

No more for now, dear.
Hope you can read my writing.
Drat these cataracts.

Frances White

PIANO BAR BLUES

Dizzy summer night
quenched with lager

her eyes dreamy
with piano bar blues

moving aside their empty glasses
his arm brushed hers

low lighting and soft cushions
made her head swim

they slipped away
into the moonlight

music fading
as they sauntered back

under the larch trees
along the water

his hands in his pockets
all the way home.

Frances White

BEST FRIEND

Your brain's
quicker than mine
you always win
at Scrabble
cryptic crosswords
your kids brighter
your house
bigger and better
than mine
your car
cruises at 90
old cat and dog
die at home
no debts
you're younger
by a couple
of years
all colours look
good on you
you suffer
no allergies
no bumps or rashes
you can still
wear stilettos
without breaking
an ankle
your husband is
dark and faithful
you've a sex life
I guess

you don't spit
venom
when you see
I've more charm
and guile
able
to disguise
my feelings
from you.
Ssss…
Ssss…

Aeronwy Thomas

DYLAN'S DAUGHTER

They want me at the party
I don't know them
they don't know me
strangers
they want me
because I'm Dylan's daughter.

Why can't my husband go
alone
they're his friends
his party
but no
they want me there too.

Can't you ring
I'm indisposed, awful cold
a bug
a severe allergy
to their kind invite.

No hope
no good prevaricating
got to bathe
prink and pother
choose an outfit
and worse
be ready on time.

"By six, did you say?"
"The earlier we get there
the earlier we can leave"
he lies
knowing the return trek
will be cold, late
lengthy.

While I'm celebrated with
Prosecco and delicious food
he'll be singing his heart out
with his Welsh friends
last to go
befuddled and sung out
with me in tow.

Ah, well
better get ready
pronto
all because I'm Dylan's daughter.

Aeronwy Thomas

SWIMMERS

Angry sea
swimming
one east one west
splashing overarm
to calmer waters
away from the swell
with words sinking
into swirls and eddies
sea weed or fish
sliding slippery
out of grasp.

Already
you're so far away
always a good swimmer
the tide turning
the words said
floatable, reachable
between heavy strokes
despite fatigue
and reluctance
to grasp again
what was said.

As my feet touch ground
in the shallows
words surface
on a rippling wave
covered with
the oil of tankers
of scum
and clinging animal life
the last words
you said to me
let's end

and I tumble on to the shore
to watch you waving
far out
at sea.

Aeronwy Thomas

VALENTINE

I send you a Valentine
with Voodoo symbols
black crosses
and bitter rue
to discourage you
no more Valentines to me
please.

Voodoo is beyond
my cultural reference
but I imagine how
ill tempered witch doctors
intent on satisfying
vengeful clients
earn their keep.

A black cross
Madonna style
must surely hint
my indifference
to your flowery Valentine
beetles hiding beneath
leaves of roses.

Remembering infidelities
attractive, suave looks
the pain inflicted

poison
rattlesnake strong
through my veins
I attach a phial
juice of rue
to my card
return the compliment.

This laden card
with blood-red hearts
as you sign
with twisted mouth
the recorded delivery
will vindicate past wrongs
my Valentine.

Aeronwy Thomas

THINKING OF LOCKERBIE

becalmed – wings clippered
all sides to port
delayed by a voyager
who loaded but forgot to board
I watch the luggage beached
black – grey – brown – dun – tan
tumbled like pebbles - and with deliberation
contemplate the prospect of the worst to happen

as a child, talismaning against catastrophe
I would conjure spiders every night
in order to avoid them in my dreams
bringing my crook'd hand towards my face – pausing –
keeping terror bayed above me in the dark

now – before we sail
onto the wide wild sea of sky
I hold up panic to try on
   DO NOT INFLATE
examine bands around the heart – and pray
that feet that once skipped pavement cracks
retain their skills – and fingers crossed are stout enough
to save us plunging through the broken clouds

Annie Taylor

MY WARTIME CHRISTMAS

Wartime Christmas at my gran's, began
with ice flowers on the window pane, and a dollies pram
at the foot of the bed, not new
'He can't get decent toys in wartime' mother said
but, stout and sturdy, rocking gently on stately springs
'He's been!' I yelled, waking my brother, he
had a pedal car in racing green, I'd seen one like it in the attic
among my father's ancient toys, Pullman cars from Hornby trains
A Bumper Book for Boys, a one winged plane.
We understood, it's wartime, Father Christmas must economize
Reindeer food was rationed, perhaps he came on foot
No lights allowed to show the way
What if guns shot down his sleigh!

Christmas Dinner at midday, Uncle Peter home on leave
great-aunties in blue dresses, gran's dried milk ice cream
listening to The King at Three, grown-ups dozy
sky rosy, A ring of the bell!
'Father Christmas, what a surprise!'
In the hall, a man in red, face shadowed by a beard and hood
'Does a little girl called Anne live here, and a lad called David
have they both been good? Here's a present each, sorry I can't stay
it's getting late, I've far to go today'
'Mum' I whispered, 'he's wearing Uncle Peter's shoes'
'Stuff and nonsense! And don't stare, it's rude!' I didn't care
for in my arms was a little house
with windows, gables, chimneys, porch
my mother flicked a switch, a torch bulb shone through every square,
no blackout curtains there, no dark nights lit alone
by gritty stars and pallid moon.
I wedged my smallest doll in the glowing door
'Nightime lights allowed! ' she said 'Here it's after the War!

Annie Taylor

DOUBLE TAKE

Shoot me Harry
With your brown brownie eyes
A last longing shot
Before you go to war
On the ten-thirty-four
Keep me in your sights
Why should I fear exposure?
Outlined by dusty daybeams
I am, after all, dressed to kill
In my sassy suit and natty hat
Your heart a pin on my lapel,
Frail smile obscured by lace
Against my shadowed face
I shall miss our last
Teary kiss, at least until
Half past six, when
I have tea at the Ritz
With an American

Annie Taylor

ONE SUMMER

We lay in meadows
among the long grasses
near the airfield.
We rolled and romped
in a sweet green sea
with singing insects.
Then, spread-eagled
in the flight path,
the warm sky hanging above
we watched the Blenheims
in patchwork browns and greens
flying so low, so close
to land, to take off.
Their shadows swept over us
our ears filled with roars.
We waved.
Hands waved back.
Grinning faces, clearly seen,
through open bomb doors.
We laughed, we screamed,
we knew nothing of wars.
Watching them fly
to unknown places
we knew nothing of dying.

Beryl Myers

PRANGED

The plane lay in the field
on its back, like a dead thing,
wings broken.
When the men had removed
what needed to be moved and had gone away
the village children came to inspect
the wreckage,
to play in the empty carcase,
its wooden ribs covered with canvas,
painted yellow.

It was dark inside, no windows
apart from the cockpit.
Wooden benches above us
where men had sat.
Boys yelled excitedly
as they wrenched instruments
away from the panel
for souvenirs, the girls too afraid to touch.

Yellow
The colour of training aircraft,
easily located.
New pilots learning
how to die.

Beryl Myers

LITTLE THOUGHTS

Little thoughts swim round my head.
It seems my body is consumed.
Cold stream water holds my legs.
Fishes nibble at my skin.
Mud squeezes up between my toes.
Who knows what hides beneath the stones
or in the dim of overhanging banks
or swims along the weeded flow.

Damp hair blows across my face.
In the air where limbs are free.
Scents of summer permeate.
Incessantly the damsel flies
skit through wands of irises.
Reaching up to feel the breeze
my body is two worlds in one.
Little thoughts swim round.

Beryl Myers

MONASTERY IN SHASTA

(to Ann)

As you say, Ann,
buddhas were my thing
Long ago
in flower-power days
we strewed petals
to honour him
sat in a lotus-like squat
no problem with knees
and emptied our minds.
No mantras, no noise,
no distraction
only Buddha
on his plinth and us
with our backs to him
our bottoms raised
on kapok cushions,
contemplating the wall.
Buddha took no offence
and finally broke
the shackles
in my mind
eased my aching joints
and made me-
just by his wooden
tranquillity -
see that I could
and would break free
from the man
who caused me
all that grief.

Aeronwy Thomas

POETRY GIVES WAY TO PRAYER

(for Aeronwy)

Your spirit wrestles with the air
life-blood drains fast in dead of night
and poetry gives way to prayer.

Wage battle in intensive care
machines and tubes invade your plight
your spirit wrestles with the air

as fragile flesh fails unaware
words have no say, eyes have no sight
and poetry gives way to prayer.

Whatever injuries you bear
the craft of words is your delight
your spirit wrestles with the air

survivor of a legend's glare
recall your voice and clear insight
as poetry gives way to prayer.

The estuary is waiting there
wrench back the tide, bring back the light
your spirit wrestles with the air
and poetry gives way to prayer.

Frances White

ROSE QUARTZ

You hold out a bowl of stones
saying, "Take one," and I choose.

Strange how a cold stone
feels so soft, looks so gentle
as rose quartz.

Stranger still that a solid stone
filters light, reveals complex veins
radiates life.

How can this stone, so small in my hand
bring warmth and comfort

soft as featherdown
        soothing as honey
                quiet as cherry blossom
                        light as a baby's breath.

Frances White

THE LAKE

Trousers rolled up, his knees
quake by the waterside.

He drowns the words
he's always heard.

Don't go too near.
Keep away from the edge.

Pool black, his eyes tell
he's ready to dive.

Matchstick arms fly out
in an arrow head.

The waters enclose him.
There's silence –

then splashing and whoops of boy
as he climbs out on the other side

ribs rippling
hair sleek as otter pelt.

Frances White

TOULOUSE OR NOT TO LOSE

How much longer
till I break free
and become a lady.

I return to this attic
in the small hours
dancing feet bruised
thighs aching from high-kick
and strip off the frills
down to underclothes and flesh
they glimpsed
but never saw the real me.

The bath tub
that's where I'd like to be
as I crawl into an unmade bed
all sweat and perfume
grabbing sleep while he stays out.

It will do for a time
dancer and concubine
till I break free
and become a lady.

Frances White

A SHADOW LAY

A shadow lay across the land
and blood was sought
when vengeance would not stay his hand.

Cruel mines lay buried in the sand
and lives were bought.
A shadow lay across the land.

Men were marked with terror`s brand,
in fear they fought
when vengeance would not stay his hand.

Though many made a gallant stand,
strife came to naught.
A shadow lay across the land.

The children did not understand;
in cross-fire caught
when vengeance would not stay his hand.

Thus a blaze of hate was fanned;
left men distraught.
A shadow lay across the land
when vengeance would not stay his hand.

Beryl Myers

MOONWOLF

Keeping watch over the skies
I look for a slice of light
to herald the coming of
the moon.

So many hours watching
in vain
eyes blinded by
stars.

You complain I ignore you
up all hours alone
what I felt for you
last full moon
belonged to that time.

I am a moonwolf
inconstant as water.

Aeronwy Thomas

ANOTHER COUNTRY

I've travelled this far
to find you've moved to
another country
I'm calling

across canyons
and valleys, mountain ridges
and the wide expanses
of the Abruzzi

and you are not here
but far away
pondering the dregs
of your glass

asking the padrone
for another
rolling your dubious cigarettes
your ear open

to demons
in a place too far
to reach
though we shout loud enough.

Aeronwy Thomas

GREYS ON GREY

There is a pigment known to Artists as Payne's Grey
Washed over other colours
Imparts a shadowed subtlety
Like a change from major to a minor key

We live in a country comfortable with greys
Early dawns, clouds before storms
Mist, sea frets, haar
Ghostly hills, layer beyond layer

'Grey' is a word of equivocation
'Shades of grey', 'grey' areas
'At night all cats are grey'
So why do we long for 'grey days to be gone?'
'Blue skies from now on?'

Annie Taylor

MYRA

(1942 – 2002)

You were lost for years
in your cloistered cul-de-sac. Youth changing
to weary middle age. Womb long empty
Heart past tears

Your brazen yellow hair had faded
to a dusty peppered brown. Hollowed
and pale those dark kohled eyes. The bloodied nightshade lips
drained to a smudged shadow

A dreary way from the barren heath
where you betrayed your kind. Did a parched tongue
still long for remembered sustenance? Your lips ache
for his putrid kiss?

Your world had also ended
among the wild crags and darkening skies
'not with a bang, but a whimper'
The whimper of a child

Annie Taylor

RED

Red is the colour of the heart
And the heart's flow
A rag to a bull, danger's light
Poppies on a pin, a cross on white
All sunsets feared or longed
All dawns false or true
The rims of much wept eyes, soft cheek's glow
Flames that warm
Infernos that consume
Scarlet women, diamond cards
The debtors scalpel line
We are all the same, sans skin
Blood is red, so we're all red within.

Annie Taylor

STREET LAMP

We look to the past
When the light shone brighter
When days were sun-filled
And after dark
We loitered hand in hand
Under its yellow beam
Your Summer dress picked out
Your face lit
In mysterious tones
As we cuddled together
Afire
Under the street lamp.

We struggle to remember
Its warm glow
Its elegant form
While the sharp lights
Where we take
Our evening stroll
These Winter nights
Are so bright
Fail to flatter
Your hard-won lines
Your worried frown.
Oh, for the street lamps
When life was just begun
And I kissed you, my love,
Under the subtle rays.

Aeronwy Thomas

DAISIES

Daisies shine in the sky at night
Spattered on a blue-black ground.
I sometimes wonder if they might
come tumbling down.

Scattered stars on the green fields lie
in the new day's dawning light
each with a gleaming golden eye,
polka-dotted white.

Beryl Myers

PAINTING THE ROOFS

Slowly, blue turns to purple
last light clings to gutters
slips over roofs
is blotted out
with daubs of neon

Town switches on
puddles, windows reflect
multi-coloured flashes
bars glow, cafes pulsate
clinking glasses
loud music, laughter

Lovers
change partners
dance, sweat, pop pills
to heart-beat rhythms
strobe-lights swing
flash fluorescent
The night is red

Beryl Myers

SQUARE PARK

Above the square park
tower blocks and window blinds
obscure her view.

In the morning rain
her dog pulls his lead, heading
for the new saplings.

She follows his path
through the flower beds, searching
for broken tulips.

No one can see how
their redness makes her heart dance
each velvet petal

smuggled in pockets
through the iron perimeter
back to the grey flat.

Fiery butterflies
spread out on her windowsill
above the square park.

Frances White

AUGUST IN BRITTANY

(2003)

Midday
piercing blue sky
hay bales scattered
not a breath of air
birds scarcely sing
apples swell
pain's pear-shaped clench
ripens and rips
the guts of summer
sun's glare penetrates
the darkest recess
leaving no doubt
of its intent
to ignite
the orchard.

Midnight
deep and blue
stars spin round
a harvest moon
inky shadows fall
under the fruit trees
cicada crescendo
splits the warm air
cider song rises
from scented branches
above
the sleeping
hay-baked
radiant
earth.

Frances White

HALLOWEEN

This is the time when the hour moves back
into the darkness, into the night
when we gain an hour and lose the light.

Now is the soggy, slippery time when
the scarecrow slumps and like it or not
the pumpkin rules the vegetable plot.

With jack-o'-lantern carried home
face carved and gouged for candlelight
the children shiver with delight.

Protected by a hollow grin
they hide their fear to trick 'n' treat
for oranges and sticky sweets.

Drawn night by night to the golden glow
their lantern sags, the young ones weep
when it's tossed outside on the compost heap.

This is the quarter that crosses the year
when hope is torn and nothing is born.
This is the time we quietly dread
the night we remember, remember the dead.

Frances White

BM

SEQUOIAS

These Methuselah trees
seem indestructible.
Regal Titans whose
high massed boughs
blank out the sun,
whose needles bed deep
the forest floor,
undisturbed for aeons
until
the roaring
searing
fires tear through.
Flames climb
monster trunks,
reduce the canopy
to fretwork,
lick round the cones
like terrorists
wreaking destruction
yet
charred cones fall
on fire-cleansed ground,
spring open to release
virile seeds into the light.
Old trees recover.
New trees take root.

Beryl Myers

SEQUOIA

THE GREEN MAN

This is the day we've waited for
the day the hour goes forward and light returns
rolling in on a green tide
as we play with time and cheat the clocks.

This is the day when the Green Man comes
from the dark wood
bearing a bonus of light across the fields
and kindles the ground with flickers of wheat.

Hear him breathe tendril and leaf
striding towards us with arms outstretched
scattering spells
and filling our land with laughter and song.

See him shine through the greening world.
Wasteland quivers with shoot and blade.
Earth is pregnant with meadow flowers.
His time has come.

This is the day we forfeit an hour
and the Green Man comes.
This is the day we've waited for.

Frances White

THE BLACK CUILLIN

What fatal error undermined your skill
when you set off without a glance behind
upon the slopes of those forbidding hills.

Escaping to the mountains and their thrill
with trusted friends you knew to be your kind
what fatal error undermined your skill.

You ventured out alone to breathe your fill
a short walk in the sunshine to unwind
upon the slopes of those forbidding hills.

The sea lay tranquil and the island still.
I wonder if their magic made you blind
as hidden peril undermined your skill.

No one was there to see you fall and spill
your youth and all the plans you had in mind
upon the slopes of those forbidding hills.

The Black Cuillin captured your free will
and shrouds the jagged facts so we can't find
what fatal error undermined your skill
upon the slopes of those forbidding hills.

Frances White

STONE

Granite set on
flowered grave
keeps evil out
defends
keeps soul beneath
interred
bright day above
black earth below
only stone is grey
with graven words to soothe
the pain of grief away

Beryl Myers

TIME AND TRANSITION

WINE AND JAM

They were getting older
his memory was failing
she was sometimes lost for words
but still they played the game of Scrabble.

Stiff backed and eager
they walked together clutching carrier bags
and made determined raids on the common
to pick fruit for home-made wine and jam.

From the first ephemeral elderflower
to the warlike barricades of bramble they foraged
until wine bubbled in the demijohns
and jam set slow for mealtimes sweet as honey.

Frances White

FERRYWISE

I decided
to walk the ferry way
to save the fare
I placed the car
on my head
and tested the water
with a toe
boots strapped
to my side.

It was freezing
but nonetheless
I stepped confidently
onto the waters
the waterway
between Sandbanks
and Purbeck.
I mustn't look down
but straight ahead
at Corfe Castle
to avoid seasickness
it was a choppy
November day.

I managed it
though the car
slid on my turban
being larger
than the usual weights
the walk on water
went just as planned
I saved £5.83
and was pleased
to have transport
the other side.

Aeronwy Thomas

PAINSHILL POETS

You blend into autumnal colours
reds, orange, yellow and brown
Sweeping boughs of trees
conceal you.
Your voice cannot be heard
above the wind
the crunch of dead leaves
the thud of chestnuts
You fight to read
your words flutter
through ruins, follies, lakes, vineyards
but leaves and poems
colours and sounds
will have their way.

Aeronwy Thomas

TEETH

I wasn't going to talk about teeth
but now you mention yours
I can tell you about mine.
It's a sad tale.
Lily-livered and travel sick
I was dragged off
the bus at Carmarthen
and frogmarched
to the dentist.
He administered gas
and I lurched into a shifting world
of crashing buses and miners' drills
waking to my mother's cries
"You've killed her,"
Then years of dentists -
everywhere - Rome, Catania, Paris.
"You've some terrible work here,"
they chorused and yanked
probed and invaded.
It's a long tale so I'll cut it short.
I lost them all.
Now, it's a question of ethics
whether or not to implant
toothsome titanium
and spend the savings
all on myself
for a porcelain smile
and delicious meals.

Aeronwy Thomas

RED HATBAND

Dashing to work
taking a short cut over Richmond Green
birdsong puts spring in my step.
Coming my way, a gentleman catches my eye
in cream trousers and a panama with a red band.

He stops to survey the listed buildings
solicitors' premises, domed theatre
Georgian terraces with magnolias filling front gardens
then leans on his stick to catch his breath.

Nearer now and clearer, his face shows pale.
No smile for me as he struggles
to make progress on home ground
the morning stroll taxing his strength.

I think of my father in his final months
wearing a checked cap for protection
from the sun. This bright day
the man with a red hatband gives me pause.
I'll stop rushing, quite so fast, to meet my deadlines.

Frances White

BALLOONS

A bunch of jolly balloons
fat and flirty
bored with the party
tired of being tied down
make their escape
with flying colours.

hustled and harried
by the winter wind
a gust thrusts them
into the tossing trees
caged by branches
they jostle together
bright cheeks squeaking
tweaked and prodded.

Soon, smooth skins will pucker
their merry bouncing falter
sad bladders dangling
like rotting fruit
wet and gaudy
till spring's green tides
envelop and hide
their once fine glory.

Annie Taylor

CHANGES

Why do they change the names?
While names are still the same
our sense of place remains
intact, our roots still tapped.

Our local swimming pool
'White City Baths'
is now 'The Janet Adegoke Leisure Centre'
taxi drivers insist on calling it "The Hokey Kokey"
but the name was born in 1908
when muddy paths, ponds and derelict farms
transiently became broad avenues, canals,
white marble walled pavilions,
vanquished in their turn
by mile on mile of brick and tiles.

Wormwood Scrubs,
yes, everybody knows the gaol,
but the name has roots as old as churchyard yews,
a time when snakes
were known as giant worms,
and the bland and open grass
a wild and lawless heath,
haunt of highway men and thieves
whose children's children's children,
still haunted,
return to this now tamed and shackled place.

And Old Oak Lane
however imprisoned and constrained
follows the perimeter of phantom fields
skirts woods transmogrified to steel and concrete,
winds beside streams descended into sewers.
So may London's lanes
buried fathoms beneath tarmacadam
still wind softly,
like half forgotten country memories
remembered in sweet melodies
sung by city birds at night
under Electric stars.

Annie Taylor

STRANGER IN CONNEMARA

The wet coast path is rough
on flimsy city shoes
blunt-nosed cars splash mud
spray stings
people speak among themselves
with opaque tongues
behind their smiles
something gleams red
like the little lamp
that flickers in the dark church
next to the dead
under their closed crosses
where plastic flowers cup the rain
in everlasting petals.

Among hillocky fields
knucklebone stones
knobble threadbare soil
the wind ferrets and tumbles
over lichened walls
shakes brambles
calls down the tall storms
that walk across the seal-backed islands
lying on rods of silver
beyond the steely sea.

Dusk sneaks up
flamingo sunset fades
turf fires smell of a thousand autumns
shadows walk the stairs
the television flickers
on the screen a softly spoken man
tells stories of implacable hatred
the turf pelt stirs on its altar of roses
old ghosts raise their heads from the hearth
like sad dogs
slipping under the door
to join the wind
keening in the tussocky grasses
hard by the shingle and the drawing tide.

Annie Taylor

RA'S JOURNEY

He rises with a flush.
Surprised to see his face
clouds blush
but as he moves apace
across the sky
clouds change from pink to grey.

Sun hanging high,
a Chinese lantern bright.
Clouds change from grey to white.
Sun sinking low.
The evening sky grows red.
Clouds now a rosy glow.

The day is dead.

Beryl Myers

OSIRIS

The green face of Osiris
surveys them as they pray
for the floods to come again,
for the dwindled Nile to rise,
to cloak the land once more
with emerald of growing crops
and gold of ripening grain,
to keep them from the locust swarms,
survive the blazing sun
until the reaping and the gleaning
will provide for everyone,
until the green face of Osiris
smiles down on them again.

Beryl Myers

THE LONG SLEEP

Dry leaves have floated from the trees,
the murmuring bees,
warm in their hive,
will stay alive.

Those hibernating butterflies,
hid from our eyes
in dusty nooks
behind old books,

keep safe while winter snow-flakes skirl.
Fat dormice curl
in grassy nests,
oblivious.

Beryl Myers

WINTER IN FIVE SENSES

Bare trees scratch the sky
With petrified fingers
Fan of blackbirds
Arch along topmost branches
A squirrel forgets to hibernate
Sits and dines brazenly
On tulip bulbs from our terracotta pots
And birdseed from squirrel-proof trays
Snowdrops point their noses out of the earth
Scenting Spring
I'll leave them all
Go indoors by the warm fire
Cosy hearing the cold drip of rain
While it collects and gurgles
Along the gutter.

Aeronwy Thomas

YEAR ROUND

Waking

Squirrel burials
resurrection
hands stretch green

Making

sand castles
pock-marked beaches
tides leave flags

Waving

Summer slips away
Acrid smoke stinks
Kids on ice

Skating

Holly prickles
bright spots of blood
robins feed

Waiting

Beryl Myers

WEATHER REPORT

The Weather lady said
"This morning
out of town is foggy,
in town
murky, damp and icky".
Does she mean dirty,
dull and sticky?
Is foggy thicky,
muggy, sicky
or froggy jumpy into puddles?
muddy wellies,
wobbly bellies
makey kiddies
dipsy, giggly.
Water drippy downy neckies.
Goshy, hecky
soaking sockies,
sloshy messes.

In town
or out it's
washy time.

Beryl Myers

BRIDGES

(for Bryan)

Bridges lead to an island
divided from the mainland
by an expanse of water.
To some, there's a continual storm,
to others it seems variable,
yet others find it calm.
The bridges were built
by men for an easier crossing,
costing many tears.
All must cross sometime.
The bridges are many.
Take one…
Don't be like the proud individual
who tried to swim…

Aeronwy Thomas

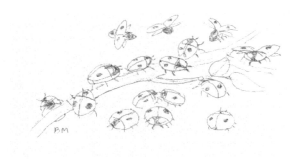

LADYBIRDS

Ladybirds, so plentiful this year,
garden pests your prey,
can we count on you next year?
No promises.

Aeronwy Thomas

CANNIBALS

He ate her with his eyes!
I watched them both with hate
And with my eyes
I ate her too.

Annie Taylor

RUSSIAN DOLL

Activity and stillness need each other.
One lives within the other
like a Russian doll.
Is stillness or activity
at the core?

Aeronwy Thomas

WHAT IS BLUE?

Deepest sea
Cloudless sky
Hills, distant and in memory
Bells that grow but never chime
Birds we seek but seldom find
Sad jazz tunes
The moon once only
And all lost lovers, adrift and lonely

Annie Taylor

WATERLILY

A waterlily extends its petals outwards
inviting a stinging bee to its breast for nectar.
What does a lily know about the sting.

Aeronwy Thomas

POT-BOUND

parlour palm potted
in temperate zone
palm potted
intemperate
potted in.

Frances White

PALM POT

They didn't know, did they
how large you would grow?
They thought their skills were
greater than God's or Nature's
(if you think God is a myth)
Such a pot they thought
would hold you tight,
you would never
escape.
Poor cracked pot.

Beryl Myers

ENSLAVED

behind the grimy glass, she keeps her place
a victim of her class
while all the precious hours pass
and shadows lengthen on the grass

Annie Taylor

NON ACTION

Non-action is also
Do not jump the gun is also
Let things take their course
Is also wisdom.

Aeronwy Thomas

THE MOON IS OUT OF REACH

the moon is out of reach

the moon is out

the moon is

the moon

is the moon

is the moon out

Is the moon out of reach

Annie Taylor

PARTING

I didn't make a scene, just waved my hand
the dockside wind was keen
how small that narrow strip of green
but all the world was in between

Annie Taylor

SUNSET

the
sun sets blood
red on the horizon
like a succulent peach laid on a blue delft dish

Beryl Myers

HORSE

After an uphill climb, we rest awhile
beneath the cool dark pine.
Sweetly shaded leisure time
wishing this hired horse were mine.

Frances White

TIGER

The world is merely phenomena
for me to sharpen my claws on.

Aeronwy Thomas

FINGERNAILS

Miss Prim and Proper
Sweet Fanny Adams to do
Perfect nail varnish

Frances White

OPAL

In a sea of denim
swayed by music, under summer skies
he wanted to buy her a diamond ring
but she chose the opal, blue
to go with her jeans.

Frances White

HAIKU

rain clatters loudly
leathery November leaves
ancient timpani

Frances White

TEARDROP

It
is a
strange
thing that
a stream of salt
water running down
the cheek can come
from deep misery
or side splitting
hilarity

Beryl Myers

EVENING PRIMROSES

Evening primroses
incandescent
in the moonlight.
Every reason
to stay out late
in my garden
tonight.

Frances White

STAR

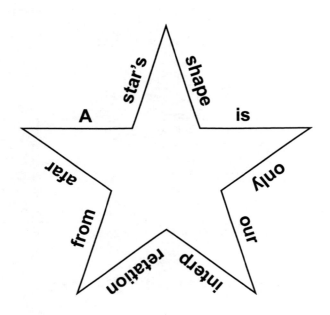

(Frances White)

NOTES TO POEMS

Aeronwy Thomas

MONASTERY IN SHASTA
Buddhist Monastery in the mountains of northern California

PAINSHILL POETS
Painshill Park, Cobham, Surrey, 18th century landscape park and garden

Annie Taylor

MARY DIBBLE
St Giles-without-Cripplegate is located in the Barbican Complex. The church was originally built without (outside) the walls of the City of London, near the Cripplegate.

VENUS OBSERVED
Acknowledgements to Diego Velasquez's 'Rockeby Venus'

DOUBLE TAKE
Acknowledgements to Bert Hardy's 'Outward Bound'

Beryl Myers

SCHOOL DINNER
This daylight raid took place in South London in 1942.

RA'S JOURNEY
Egyptian Sun God

OSIRIS
Egyptian God of life, death, resurrection, and fertility, influencing the fertile flooding of the Nile River and growth of vegetation.

Frances White

THE BLACK CUILLIN
A range of rocky mountains on the Isle of Skye in Scotland

AUGUST IN BRITTANY
The 2003 heat wave caused high mortality rates in Paris and other cities in France.

POETRY GIVES WAY TO PRAYER
Written for Aeronwy during a period of illness

TOULOUSE OR NOT TO LOSE
Acknowledgements to Toulouse Lautrec's 'Femme à sa toilette'

ACKNOWLEDGEMENTS

Some of the poems in Away With Words
first appeared in the following publications:

Aeronwy Thomas
Later Than Laugharne - Celtion 1977
Nightride And Sunrise, ed. Edward Lobury - Celtion 1978,
Poetry Monthly 2005
Burning Bridges, ed. Stanley Barkan - Cross Cultural Communications,
New York, (forthcoming publication)

Annie Taylor
Scope - RACC Poetry Society,1995,1996, 1997 & 1998
poetrymonthly.com, Issue 130 - January 2007
A Time to Remember and Give Thanks for our Children, 2007
Guy's and St Thomas' NHS Trust

Beryl Myers
Some of these poems have appeared in:
Patchwork - Whatley Writers Press
Red Tomatoes - Whatley Writers Press
poetrymonthly.com - issue 127, October 2006
Openings 24 - 2007 Open University Press

Frances White
Scope 1996 - Poetry Society, Richmond Adult Community College
This Is My Voice 1998, 2000, 2001 - Waterstone's
Kingston University Bookshop
The Osterley Poetry Trail, Love Poems in the Park 2004 - The National Trust
poetrymonthly.com, Issue 127 - October 2006
A Time to Remember and Give Thanks for our Children, 2007- Guy's
and St Thomas' NHS Trust